"**There is no** doubt **about precisely when folks** started **racing each othe**r **in automo**bile. It **was the day the**y **built the** second **automobile.**"

—*Richard Petty*

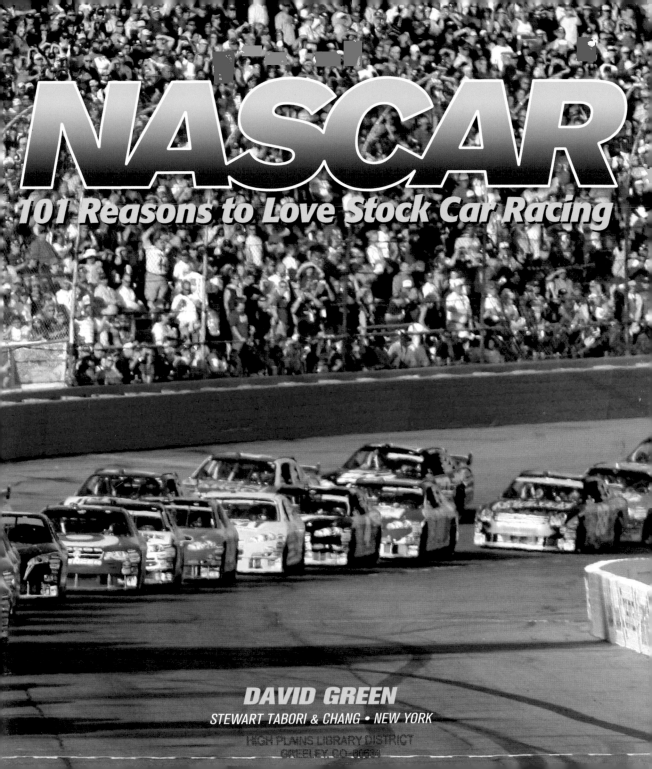

NASCAR

101 Reasons to Love Stock Car Racing

DAVID GREEN

STEWART TABORI & CHANG • NEW YORK

INTRODUCTION

The first stock car race I ever saw was on a poorly lit half-mile clay track. The drivers wore blue jeans or work pants and T-shirts, and the crowd wore a layer of red dust kicked up in a big cloud by the racers. They blew tires, knocked down fences, hit light poles, wrecked, and raced hard—and when it was over, sometimes they fought, or sometimes they just took a swig from a liquor bottle and hoped the promoter had stuck around to pay them off.

I loved it, and through all the years that have followed, through the sport's transformation into a rich, flashy, high-tech operation, I've continued to be fascinated by it.

How can you not love a sport in which you find nicknames like Fireball, Speedy, Coo Coo, Handsome Harry, Chargin' Charlie, the King, the Rainbow Warriors, and Smoke, and whose nominal guru is a latter-day Barnum called Humpy?

It's a sport born on dark, twisting mountain back roads with jacked-up Fords loaded with white lightning and lawmen in hot pursuit.

It's a sport in which drivers are so good at their work that they can drive hundreds of miles in traffic at speeds approaching 200 miles per hour, in cars crafted by brilliant technicians.

Author's Note:
This book focuses on NASCAR's top division, currently known as the Sprint Cup Series. Prior to the Sprint Cup, the series was known as the Strictly Stock division (1949), the Grand National division (1950-1971), the Winston Cup (1972-2003), and the Nextel Cup (2004-2007). Any reference to Cup races refers to these.

At its heart, stock car racing is still a sport with hair on its chest, as it was in the red clay and mountain road days, and, as we sometimes see in the grandstands, hair on its back, too. It's still a beer sport, a fried chicken sport, a pickup truck sport—but that's only at its core.

On the surface, it is a huge, slick, multimillion-dollar production every week of the season, drawing enormous crowds and big-name sponsors with deep pockets.

Where once it was all homemade speed, reckless bravery, and folksy charm, now it has glamour, the kind of glamour—and payday—that has attracted Indianapolis 500 winners to it. It has spread across the country and shot up the TV charts. Movies have been made about it. Leno and Letterman host drivers on their shows.

The sport has come a long way. The days of shade tree mechanics (knuckle busters) and weekend warriors have evolved into sprawling high-tech garages with dozens of cars being prepared in them and drivers who fly their own planes, live in huge homes, and vacation in Portofino.

But when the green flag drops and 43 cars come roaring down the straightaway, side by side, bumper to bumper, sounding like a tornado, setting hearts to pounding, none of that matters. It's just racing, simple as that, racing just like it's always been, men taking risks to get there first.

This book, written and designed by my son David, will tell its story and make you want a seat at the start-finish line.

—Ron Green Sr.
  sportswriter and columnist

This book is dedicated to "Papa" Roy Green and "Granddaddy" John Griffin, two champions with hearts of gold.

Jeff Gordon

"GENTLEMEN, START YOUR ENGINES"

These are the most anticipated words at every race. Upon receiving the command from the starter, drivers fire up their engines and prepare for teeth-gnashin', steering-wheel-chokin', paint-swappin', rubber-burnin', heart-stoppin' battle. And they're just gettin' started.

2 "BOOGITY, BOOGITY, BOOGITY…"

"Let's go racin', boys!" That's three-time Cup champion and Fox broadcaster Darrell Waltrip's call from the booth when the green flag is dropped on a race.

Red Farmer (61), 1953

"Cars came roaring down the road, turned left, and raced toward the beach. They would hit sand blown onto the road, lose control, fly over the retaining wall, and disappear down a hill. There must have been five or six cars down there, one piling on top of another. And I thought, these guys are crazy."

–Ron Green

3 RACIN' ON THE BEACH

In 1936, in Daytona Beach, Florida, officials decided to hold a race for street-legal family cars on the same stretch of sand where Sir Malcolm Campbell had piloted his rocket car in his attempts to set new land speed records for automobiles in previous years. The 3.2-mile course ran up the beach for approximately a mile and a half, made a sharp 180-degree turn around a large sandbank, and then ran back down Highway A1A, where another turn took racers off the asphalt and back onto the beach.

Milt Marion won the scheduled 250-mile event after it was stopped three laps early because cars were getting stuck in the sand. Bill France Sr., who would later found the National Association of Stock Car Auto Racing (NASCAR), finished fifth. Unfortunately for the town of Daytona Beach, the race was a financial disaster, and the town left the promotion and sponsorship of future races to others.

This didn't deter Bill France, however. After the local Elks club sponsored the 1937 race, France convinced restaurateur Charlie Reese to put up the money for a 150-mile event in 1938. Smokey Purser beat France and Lloyd Moody to the finish line, but he was found to have changed the cylinder heads on his engine, resulting in his disqualification for illegally altering his "stock" car. France awarded Moody the victory to avoid any controversy arising from declaring himself the winner.

The racing could get wild on the beach, with cars crashing into the waves and careening through the sand-banked turns, and it became more and more popular. Except for the years during World War II, racing continued on Daytona Beach through 1958. Paul Goldsmith won the last race on the beach, outrunning Curtis Turner in a spirited sprint to the checkered flag. When France opened Daytona International Speedway the next year, he moved the races to the high-banked, 2.5-mile paved track.

4 BIG BILL

In 1935, in search of a warmer climate and steadier work, Bill France Sr. withdrew his life savings, $75, from the bank, purchased $50 worth of tools, packed his wife and young son into his car, and headed for Florida. France earned extra cash for the trip by working on broken-down cars along the way. The family settled in Daytona Beach, where France took a job at the local Pontiac-Cadillac dealership.

An imposing figure at six feet five inches and 220 pounds, France was known as "Big Bill." His love of racing was as big as he was—maybe bigger. He worked on race cars and even drove his own when he had the opportunity, joining the town of Daytona Beach in organizing and promoting local racing events.

France's vision led to the creation of NASCAR in 1947, as well as the construction of Daytona International Speedway and later Alabama International Motor Speedway (now named Talladega Superspeedway). He was tireless in his promotion of the sport. NASCAR continued to grow bigger and bigger, and today it stands as a testament to France's vision and determination.

5 THE BIRTH OF NASCAR

Big Bill France was frustrated with the lack of organization in stock car racing. There were too many groups involved and no clear leadership when he brought 35 owners and drivers together in the Ebony Room of the Streamline Hotel in Daytona Beach in December 1947. After three days of discussion, the group agreed to form NASCAR and named France president. More than 60 years later, France's dream is bigger and better than even he imagined it could be.

Left: Bill France Sr. at Daytona International Speedway

Red Byron won the very first race at Martinsville
Speedway, on September 7, 1947.

6 RED BYRON

Robert Byron earned the nickname "Red" driving the dirt tracks of Alabama in the late 1930s and early 1940s. When World War II broke out, Byron enlisted in the Army Air Corps where he served as a tail gunner on a B-24. Byron's plane was shot down over the Aleutian Islands during his 58th mission, and he was lucky to survive, suffering severe injuries to his left leg that required several surgeries and two years spent in and out of hospitals. Eventually Byron was able to return to racing, winning the first official NASCAR-sanctioned event driving Ray Park's Ford at Daytona Beach in 1948. Because of his injuries, he had to drive the race with his left foot bolted to the clutch. Byron won the Modified division's points championship that year and then won the first Strictly Stock championship in 1949. Byron was named one of NASCAR's "50 Greatest Drivers of All Time" in 1998.

7 SMALL-TOWN ROOTS

NASCAR is big time now, but its roots are in the small towns of the Southeast. Towns like Ronda, North Carolina; Hueytown, Alabama; and Floyd, Virginia. And at local tracks like those in Hillsborough and North Wilkesboro, North Carolina; Lakewood, Georgia; Lancaster, South Carolina; and Martinsville, Virginia. In fact, NASCAR has been racing at Martinsville Speedway, the shortest track in the Cup series at .526 mile, since 1948—longer than any other track currently in the circuit.

> "They told me if I saw a red flag to stop. They didn't say anything about the checkered flag. . . . They finally threw the red flag and I pulled in. I had finished third."
>
> —Louise Smith

8 STRICTLY STOCK... OR NOT

NASCAR's Strictly Stock series made its debut in 1949, only to be renamed the Grand National series a year later. Glenn Dunaway, driving a Ford, won the first race at a bumpy dirt track on the west side of Charlotte, North Carolina. A post-race inspection revealed that Dunaway had illegally modified his rear springs, resulting in disqualification. Second-place Jim Roper, who finished three laps back in the 150-mile race, was declared the winner. It seems that this type of controversy was fairly common in NASCAR's early years.

9 THE GOOD OL' GAL

Louise Smith could drive. Back in the 1940s and 1950s, she drove in Modified, Sportsman, and even NASCAR Grand National events (NASCAR'S top level at the time), winning 38 times on the junior circuits. Known as the "Good Ol' Gal," Smith was recruited by Bill France Sr. to drive in a race at Greenville Pickens Speedway in South Carolina as a way of attracting more fans to the track, particularly women. In her first race, she was told to keep driving unless she saw a red flag stopping the race. But when the race ended, she just kept going. No one had told her she could also stop when the checkered flag dropped. The hard-charging pioneer, who was well known for her ability to outrun the law on the back roads of South Carolina, didn't stop for good until she retired in 1956. Smith, who passed away in 2006, was the first woman inducted into the International Motorsports Hall of Fame, in 1999.

The first NASCAR Strictly Stock race, in Charlotte, North Carolina, June 19, 1949.

Johnny Mantz (98) brings up the rear of the pack at the start of the 1950 Southern 500 at Darlington Raceway

10 TOO TOUGH TO TAME

Most folks thought he was crazy, but Harold Brasington had a dream. Inspired by a visit to Indianapolis Motor Speedway, Brasington set out to build his own paved superspeedway in 1949, in rural Darlington, South Carolina. Figuring he could attract drivers from the newly formed stock car racing association known as NASCAR, Brasington picked out a patch of land and started building. The result was Darlington Raceway, the meanest, most capricious 1.366 miles you'd ever want to meet. Distinctively egg-shaped because landowner Sherman Ramsey didn't want his minnow pond disturbed, the "Track Too Tough to Tame" is legendary for its difficulty, with a racing groove so narrow, many cars end up with the "Darlington Stripe"—paint scraped off their right side. It's a true test of skill and determination, with a bit of chance mixed in, and drivers learn very quickly not to mess with "the Lady in Black."

11 SLOW AND STEADY

The very first Southern 500, run at Darlington Raceway during Labor Day weekend in 1950, featured a field of 75 cars that started three wide. It was NASCAR's first event on a paved track and first 500-mile race. Johnny "Madman" Mantz, driving a Plymouth co-owned by NASCAR founder Bill France Sr., was the last to qualify—nearly 10 miles per hour slower than pole winner Curtis Turner. Mantz, drawing on his experience in open-wheel racing at Indianapolis, knew the surface would chew up the softer tires normally used on NASCAR's dirt tracks and shrewdly chose to run the race with harder truck tires. While the faster cars shredded tire after tire, Mantz steadily cruised around the track down on the apron. He won the race by nine laps over second-place Fireball Roberts, at an average speed of just over 75 miles per hour.

12 THE BEST DAMN GARAGE IN TOWN

That's the name of the garage Smokey Yunick ran on Beach Street in Daytona Beach from 1947 to 1987. "The Best Damn Race Car Mechanic" was hired by team owner Marshall Teague to prepare Herb Thomas' "Fabulous Hudson Hornet" for the second running of the Southern 500 at Darlington, in 1951. Thomas won the race and went on to win the first of two points championships that year. Yunick enjoyed great success in the racing world, building cars for Fireball Roberts, Marvin Panch, and Bobby Isaac, to name a few, as well as fielding cars in the Indianapolis 500.

13 SMOKEY'S BAG OF TRICKS

Among the most infamous of Yunick's creative efforts to skirt NASCAR's rules was installing a coiled fuel line in his Chevrolet that was 11-feet long and two inches in diameter, and held several extra gallons of gasoline. At the time, NASCAR had limits on the size of the gas tank, but not the fuel line. When inspectors stripped the tank out of Yunick's Chevelle after a race to verify that it met regulations, Yunick was able to drive back to his garage on the gas remaining in his fuel line.

However, even that pales in comparison to what Yunick did in 1966. Curtis Turner's No. 13 Chevelle, built by Yunick, was so much faster than the competition in practice that NASCAR officials were convinced it didn't fit the stock car profile required. But on initial inspection, officials found nothing wrong. After further investigation, NASCAR determined that Yunick had built an exact replica of the stock car at seven-eighths scale, making it dramatically lighter and faster than the competition. Brilliant!

"All those other guys were cheatin' ten times worse than us, so it was just self-defense."
−Smokey Yunick

Herb Thomas and Smokey Yunick

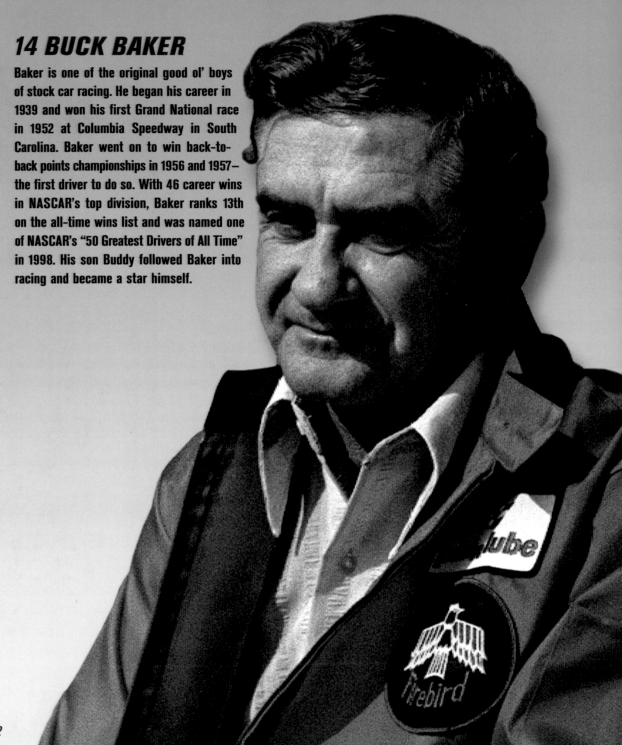

14 BUCK BAKER

Baker is one of the original good ol' boys of stock car racing. He began his career in 1939 and won his first Grand National race in 1952 at Columbia Speedway in South Carolina. Baker went on to win back-to-back points championships in 1956 and 1957—the first driver to do so. With 46 career wins in NASCAR's top division, Baker ranks 13th on the all-time wins list and was named one of NASCAR's "50 Greatest Drivers of All Time" in 1998. His son Buddy followed Baker into racing and became a star himself.

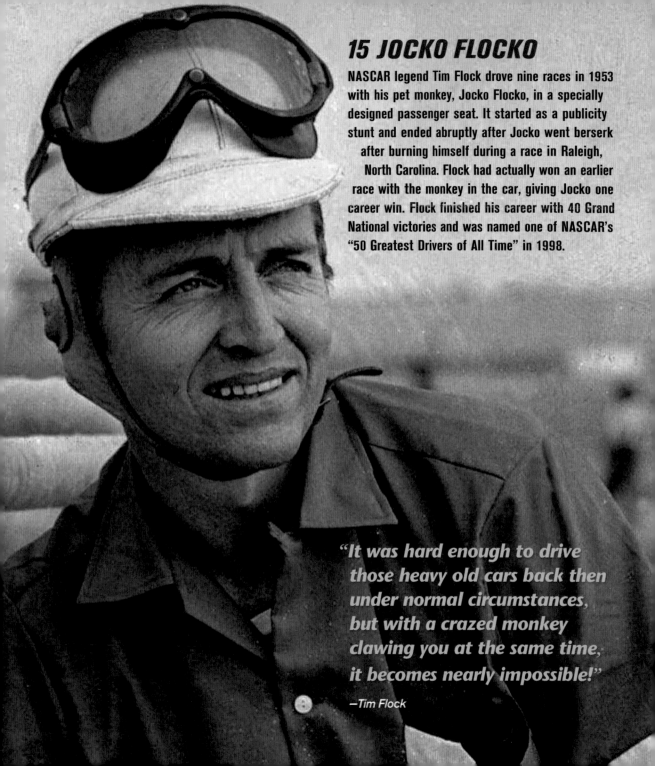

15 JOCKO FLOCKO

NASCAR legend Tim Flock drove nine races in 1953 with his pet monkey, Jocko Flocko, in a specially designed passenger seat. It started as a publicity stunt and ended abruptly after Jocko went berserk after burning himself during a race in Raleigh, North Carolina. Flock had actually won an earlier race with the monkey in the car, giving Jocko one career win. Flock finished his career with 40 Grand National victories and was named one of NASCAR's "50 Greatest Drivers of All Time" in 1998.

"It was hard enough to drive those heavy old cars back then under normal circumstances, but with a crazed monkey clawing you at the same time, it becomes nearly impossible!"

—Tim Flock

Curtis Turner, Daytona, 1956

16 CURTIS TURNER

Turner may have been the quintessential stock car driver. Brazenly independent, he liked to drive fast and party hard. Best buddies with Joe Weatherly, Pops Turner left an indelible mark on NASCAR history. In 1958, he announced plans to build a track just north of Charlotte, North Carolina, eventually teaming with race promoter Bruton Smith, who had similar plans. They broke ground in 1959, and Charlotte Motor Speedway was born.

Turner won only 17 races on NASCAR's senior circuit, but that was partly due to the fact that Bill France Sr. issued him a lifetime ban in 1961 for attempting to organize a drivers' union. Turner was reinstated in 1965 and went on to win the American 500 at North Carolina Speedway—the first race at the new track in Rockingham. He died in 1970 when the plane he was piloting crashed in Pennsylvania.

17 HOLD ON!

Back in the late 1950s, Curtis Turner drove the pace car for a Grand National race at the Charlotte Fairgrounds—a classic half-mile dirt track on the north edge of town. Turner, driving a Ford convertible from a local dealer, wasn't competing in the race and asked sportswriter Max Muhleman to ride along. But after completing the pace laps, Turner decided to stay on the track when the green flag fell and "make a lap" ahead of the field. The stunt didn't go over well with front-row starters Buck Baker and Speedy Thompson, who tried to chase him down, nor did it sit well with Muhleman, who hung on for dear life in the back seat. Apparently, though, Turner enjoyed the heck out of it.

"It was an act of God that I didn't go out of the car in one of the turns before Curtis, grinning happily, finally pulled in."

—Max Muhleman on his ride with Curtis Turner

18 FIREBALL ROBERTS

Born in Daytona Beach in 1929, Edward Glenn Roberts Jr. earned the nickname "Fireball" for the crackling fastball he threw as a youngster—but he made his name in stock car racing. Roberts finished second to Bill Rexford in his rookie season on the Grand National circuit in 1950. Over the course of a 15-year career, Roberts won 33 times, with a career-high of eight wins in 1957, and was at his best on the big tracks. He won four times at Darlington—the Rebel 300 in 1957 and 1959, and the Southern 500 in 1958 and 1963—and six times at Daytona International Speedway. Roberts swept both races at Daytona in 1962, making him the first driver to win both events in the same year. It was his only win in the 500. Despite this success, Roberts never won a points championship. He died in 1964 from injuries sustained in a fiery crash at Charlotte Motor Speedway. Roberts was named one of NASCAR's "50 Greatest Drivers of All Time" in 1998.

19 THE CLOWN PRINCE

Joe Weatherly, known as "the clown prince of stock car racing," was one of NASCAR's great characters. Good buddies with Curtis Turner, Weatherly drove fast and partied hard. He constantly played practical jokes, once wearing a Peter Pan suit during practice, or so the story goes. He won 25 races on NASCAR's Grand National circuit from 1956 to 1964, winning back-to-back Cup championships in 1962 and 1963, driving for Bud Moore. Weatherly was killed in a crash at Riverside International Raceway in 1964. Darlington Raceway paid tribute to him by naming its museum the Joe Weatherly Stock Car Museum. Weatherly was named one of NASCAR's "50 Greatest Drivers of All Time" in 1998.

"*He was just what the sport needed at the time.*"

—Ned Jarrett on Fireball Roberts

Fireball Roberts, left, and Joe Weatherly

20 DAYTONA

A monument to Big Bill France's vision, Daytona International Speedway is the sport's grandest stage, its Olympus, its heaven. There is no choir, just the haunting echo of cars hurrying around the track with brave men at the wheel, chasing glory.

Everything seems bigger here. The 2.5-mile tri-oval, which opened in 1959, features turns that are banked at a 31-degree angle and a back straightaway that stretches for 3,000 feet, allowing today's driver to reach speeds in excess of 200 miles per hour.

This is where history is made twice a year—in the season-opening spectacle known as the Daytona 500 and the 400-mile race every July. NASCAR's best drivers come to the track in search of that elusive career-defining moment that will forever place them among NASCAR's elite. These triumphs and tragedies define the sport, forever etched in our memories. This is Daytona.

21 ANNIE'S ARMY

Bill France's wife, Anne, was named secretary and treasurer of NASCAR in 1947 and moved into the same role at Daytona International Speedway before it opened in 1959. Among her many important duties was running the speedway's ticket office. The group that worked for her there became known as "Annie's Army."

Juanita "Lightnin'" Epton was a charter member of Annie's Army, manning the ticket window when the track opened—and she's still there. Nicknamed "Lightnin'" by her husband because he said he never knew when she was going to strike, Epton has been a part of NASCAR's family for 50 incredible years.

Firecracker 250, 1960

"There have been other tracks that separated the men from the boys. This is the track that will separate the brave from the weak after the boys are gone."

–Jimmy Thompson

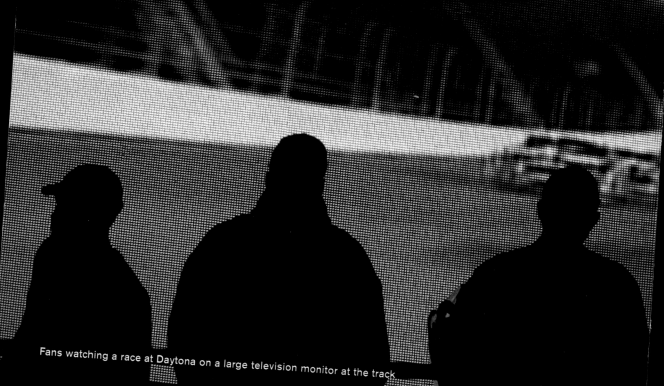

Fans watching a race at Daytona on a large television monitor at the track.

THE GREAT AMERICAN RACE

The Super Bowl of racing, the Daytona 500 is the most coveted title in all of NASCAR. Contrary to most sports, this most prestigious event is the first race of the NASCAR Sprint Cup season, not the last. The 200-lap race has a history of fantastic finishes, starting with the very first race in 1959. And it's seen its share of tragedy, including the death of NASCAR legend Dale Earnhardt in 2001.

Some drivers have enjoyed amazing success at Daytona. Richard Petty won the 500 seven times. And others have struggled for years to break through. It took Darrell Waltrip 17 tries. Buddy Baker finally won in his 18th start. And Dale Earnhardt failed 19 times before claiming his only victory, in 1998.

And it has also become staggeringly popular. These days more than 150,000 fans fill the stands for the race, with an estimated 80,000 more in the infield. And more than ten million homes in the United States are typically tuned in to watch the race on television, making it one of the most watched sporting events of the year.

23 THE PATRIARCH

The Petty name is synonymous with NASCAR. The first of four generations of race car drivers, Lee Petty was there when NASCAR ran the first officially sanctioned Strictly Stock race in 1949 at Charlotte Speedway and won his first Cup race later that year at Heidelberg Raceway in Pittsburgh. Petty claimed his first points championship in 1954 and added two more, in 1958 and 1959, making him the first driver to win it three times.

The inaugural Daytona 500 was held on February 22, 1959. A field of 59 cars took to the track for the first of what has become a multitude of unforgettable races. Not surprisingly, given the previous history of stock car racing, the three-hour-and-41-minute race ended with a bit of controversy. Lee Petty and Johnny Beauchamp crossed the line side by side with the lapped car of Joe Weatherly. Both drivers cruised into Victory Lane, where Beauchamp was declared the winner. Petty believed he had won the race and protested. It took three days to sort things out. Photos were collected from around the country, and it was finally determined that Petty had won by a mere two feet.

A terrible accident in a qualifying race at Daytona in 1961 sent Petty's car airborne after crashing through the guardrail. It nearly killed Petty, and he wasn't the same driver afterward. Still, Petty won 54 times before he retired in 1964 to concentrate on the business side of racing. With sons Richard and Maurice, he founded Petty Enterprises, the most successful race team in the history of NASCAR. Petty was named one of NASCAR's "50 Greatest Drivers of All Time" in 1998.

Lee Petty (42) and Johnny Beauchamp (73),
1959 Daytona 500

"I figure you get out of life just about what you put into it."

–Lee Petty

The green flag drops at Darlington.
Inset: Fans enjoy a dip in the infield.

24 THE EXPERIENCE

Some folks park their RV in the middle of the infield and spend the entire week at the track, complete with lounge chairs, TV, and whatever else one might take on vacation. Others show up on race day with coolers full of beer and homemade fried chicken, and sit among the tens of thousands of fans in the grandstand. They wait in the rain or bake in the blistering sun to see and feel the thundering herd of cars roar past, lap after lap, and return home exhilarated and exhausted, awash in the sights, sounds, and smells of a day at the track. It's an experience like no other in sports.

RED, WHITE, AND BLUE

The spirit of patriotism on display at every NASCAR event is nothing short of amazing. From the exuberant pre-race festivities, to team sponsorship by branches of the armed forces, and on to the passionate devotion and faith of dedicated fans—red, white, and blue are the primary colors of NASCAR.

LOYALTIES

It seems like just about everything in NASCAR has some kind of logo or decal on it. Drivers are sure to mention their sponsors every chance they get. Try keeping count during an interview. And the fans are some of the most brand-loyal around. Studies have shown, time and again, that fans tend to buy what their favorite driver advertises—and they stick with it.

"**People don't make road trips to NASCAR races. They make pilgrimages.**"

—*Monte Dutton, from* Haul A** and Turn Left:
The Wit and Wisdom of NASCAR

Pre-race ceremonies at Richmond

27 THE LAST AMERICAN HERO

Junior Johnson learned to drive running moonshine from the foothills of North Carolina down to larger towns like Charlotte. While it may not be the kind of history that NASCAR is particularly proud of, Johnson is more than happy to talk about it. His aggressive driving style and knowledge of cars came from those early days after World War II racing down back roads with a trunk-load of illicit corn liquor.

From 1953 to 1966, Johnson won 50 Winston Cup races, including 13 in 1965, tying him for eighth on the all-time list with Ned Jarrett. When he was done driving, Johnson put together his own team and won six championships in the 1970s and 1980s with drivers Cale Yarborough and Darrell Waltrip. Johnson was one the sharpest, most intelligent men in racing. His teams were often dominant and always competitive. All told, his drivers won 139 races in the Winston and Nextel Cup Series.

In 1964, white-suited author Tom Wolfe wrote "The Last American Hero," a 20,000-word essay for *Esquire* magazine that told the story of Junior Johnson and his rise from a moonshine runner to one of NASCAR's legends. The story introduced Johnson and NASCAR to a large new audience as the sport began its ascent into the mainstream.

Johnson sold his team and retired in 1995 to his farm, just five miles from where he got his start, in Ronda, North Carolina. He was named one of NASCAR's "50 Greatest Drivers of All Time" in 1998.

28 FEELIN' A DRAFT

When Junior Johnson showed up at the 1960 Daytona 500, he knew his Chevy couldn't keep up with the much faster Pontiacs, which included the one driven by pole sitter Cotton Owens. But in practice, Johnson slid in right behind Owens and discovered his car could run with Owens' Pontiac as long as he stayed right on Owens' rear bumper. Johnson had inadvertently discovered what became known as the "aerodynamic draft," and he used this newfound wisdom in the ensuing race. When the rear window popped out of leader Bobby Johns' car with 10 laps to go, Johnson swept by Johns' spinning car and went on to claim his only Daytona 500 victory.

"Moonshiners put more time, energy, thought, and love into their cars than any racer ever will. Lose on the track, and you go home. Lose with a load of whiskey, and you go to jail."

–Junior Johnson

Junior Johnson

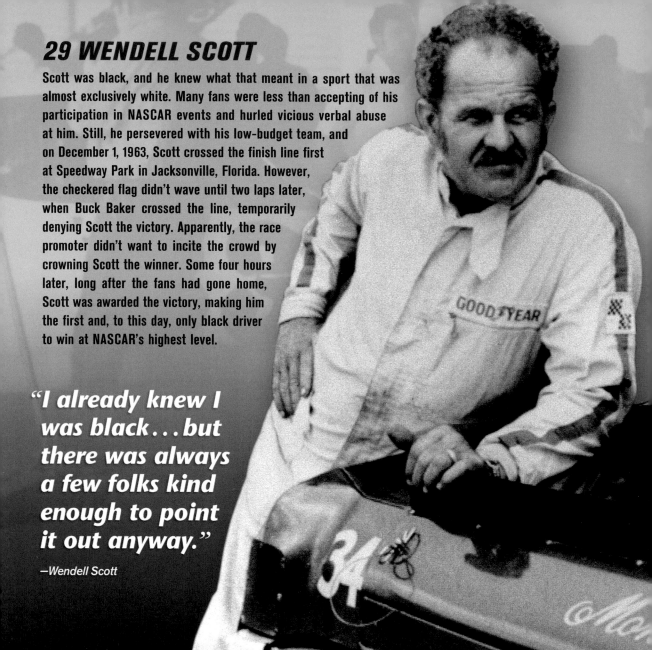

29 WENDELL SCOTT

Scott was black, and he knew what that meant in a sport that was almost exclusively white. Many fans were less than accepting of his participation in NASCAR events and hurled vicious verbal abuse at him. Still, he persevered with his low-budget team, and on December 1, 1963, Scott crossed the finish line first at Speedway Park in Jacksonville, Florida. However, the checkered flag didn't wave until two laps later, when Buck Baker crossed the line, temporarily denying Scott the victory. Apparently, the race promoter didn't want to incite the crowd by crowning Scott the winner. Some four hours later, long after the fans had gone home, Scott was awarded the victory, making him the first and, to this day, only black driver to win at NASCAR's highest level.

> "I already knew I was black...but there was always a few folks kind enough to point it out anyway."
>
> —Wendell Scott

30 TINY TO THE RESCUE

Prior to the 1963 Daytona 500, Marvin Panch was running practice laps for a sports car race when his Maserati burst into flames after a crash. DeWayne "Tiny" Lund, who was in the infield at the time, rushed to the crash and pulled Panch from the burning car, saving his life. The hospitalized Panch then asked the Wood brothers, owners of the car he was to drive in the Daytona 500, to let Lund drive in his place. As a fitting reward for his heroic deed, Lund won the race—one of only five Cup victories in a 21-year career. Amazingly, he did it on a single set of tires—unheard of in this day and age.

Ned Jarrett, center, with Vicki Johnson, Miss Southern 500, left, and Jarrett's wife, Martha, 1965. Inset: Jarrett (11) avoiding trouble at Darlington, 1962.

31 GENTLEMAN NED

In his early years, Ned Jarrett often drove using another name because his father had forbidden him to race. Eventually his father caught on after Jarrett won a race at the local track in Hickory, North Carolina, and told him to start using his own name. Jarrett's father reasoned that if young Ned insisted on disobeying his father, he might as well get proper credit by using his real name. Jarrett went on to win 50 races on NASCAR's Grand National circuit in the 1950s and 1960s, including a career-best 15 in 1964. He won the 1965 Southern 500 at Darlington Raceway by a NASCAR-record 14 laps. Known as "Gentlemen Ned" for his pleasant and respectful demeanor, Jarrett also claimed two Grand National points championships, in 1961 and 1965. In 1966, Jarrett decided to retire from racing at the relatively young age of 34. He later became a successful TV analyst and gave a memorably emotional account of his son Dale's first victory in the Daytona 500, in 1993. Jarrett was named one of NASCAR's "50 Greatest Drivers of All Time" in 1998.

32 RACESTOPPERS

In earlier years, when a winning driver pulled into Victory Lane, he would typically find himself flanked by one or two beauty queens who planted kisses on the lucky driver as he received his trophy. These lovely ladies were called Racestoppers.

33 THE KING

Where does one start when singing the praises of Richard Petty, the undisputed "King" of stock car racing? His 200 career wins are the most ever by a NASCAR driver—95 more than David Pearson, who's second on the list with 105.

Son of Lee Petty, patriarch of the Petty racing family, Richard began his career at the age of 21, in 1958. He was named Rookie of the Year in 1959, and he won the first of his seven points championships In 1964. Petty also won a record seven Daytona 500s. He recorded a ridiculous 712 top-ten finishes in 1,184 races started and leads just about every major category in NASCAR's record books for Cup drivers. Petty's red and blue No. 43 became one of the enduring icons of stock car racing.

A fierce competitor on the track, Petty is loved by fans for his unassuming manner and engaging personality. He became the sport's biggest star at the same time it was expanding beyond its regional bounds. The King still heads up Petty Enterprises today and remains one of the great ambassadors of the sport. And, of course, he was named one of NASCAR's "50 Greatest Drivers of All TIme" in 1998.

"I'd rather be called the King than other things I've been called."
—Richard Petty

34 THE KING'S 1967 SEASON

Richard Petty's numbers from his 1967 season are staggering. In 48 starts, he won 27 times—27!—including a record 10 straight, and 15 of 18 between August 12 and October 1. Petty also finished second seven times. He held the lead at some point in 41 of those 48 races and won his only Southern 500 at Darlington Raceway that year. This dominant performance earned Petty the second of his record-tying seven points championships.

35 PETTY BLUE

Without a doubt, the shade of blue that adorns the No. 43 car originally driven by Richard Petty is one of the most recognizable in all of NASCAR. According to Petty, the color was a result of a compromise. Apparently the boys in the shop didn't have enough dark blue or white paint to cover the entire race car, so they mixed them together—the result, a sky blue shade forever known as "Petty Blue."

> **"When you're looking at me, you're looking at NASCAR history."**
> –Richard Petty

36 THE SILVER FOX

David Pearson ranks second to Richard Petty in all-time Cup wins with 105. The "Silver Fox" won three Winston Cup points championships, in 1966, '68, and '69. And in 1973, Pearson won 11 races in just 18 starts, but lost the points championship to Benny Parsons, who won only one race that year. Pearson also won an unprecedented 11 consecutive poles at Charlotte Motor Speedway from 1973 to 1978. Pearson is best known for his years in the No. 21 Purolator Mercury owned by the Wood brothers. He won 43 races for them in a seven-year stretch, from 1972 to 1979. Pearson is without a doubt one of the best drivers in the history of NASCAR and was honored as one of NASCAR's "50 Greatest Drivers of All Time" in 1998.

37 PETTY AND PEARSON

The rivalry that developed between Richard Petty and David Pearson was the most competitive NASCAR has ever seen. Between 1964 and 1975, they won nine of twelve Winston Cup points championships. Sixty-three times they finished first and second in races run from 1963 to 1977, with Pearson winning 33 and Petty 30. It doesn't get any better than that.

One of the most memorable races was the 1974 Firecracker 400 at Daytona. Pearson led Richard Petty across the line as they took the white flag, signaling the final lap. As Pearson sped into the backstretch with Petty all over his tail, everyone knew Petty would attempt to slingshot past Pearson—but Pearson lifted off the gas and dove onto the apron, feigning engine trouble, as Petty shot past. Everyone was fooled, including Petty, as the Silver Fox slid in right behind the No. 43 car and gave Petty a taste of his own medicine, speeding past Petty to beat him to the checkered flag. It was a brilliant move that earned Pearson enormous respect and Petty's ire.

David Pearson takes the checkered flag ahead of Richard Petty in the 1974 Firecracker 400 at Daytona. Inset: David Pearson

"It's like you're sitting in the middle of a parking lot. This parking lot just happens to be going really, really fast."

–Ken Schrader on Talladega

38 TALLADEGA

It's the biggest, fastest track in NASCAR. Talladega Superspeedway, built and owned by the France family's International Speedway Corporation, opened in 1969 as Alabama International Motor Speedway. The 2.66-mile tri-oval course features turns banked at a mind-bending 33 degrees and a 4,000-foot back straightaway.

Anticipating catastrophe due to the high speeds and unreliable tires, members of the Professional Drivers Association, led by Richard Petty, boycotted the first Grand National race. NASCAR president Bill France Sr. was unbowed and ran the race as planned, breaking the back of the proposed union. Richard Brickhouse won—his only win in the Grand National series.

Speed has always been Talladega's trademark. Buddy Baker was the first to qualify at a speed of more than 200 mph, in 1970, and Rusty Wallace set a record for a closed oval course by turning a practice lap at 216.309 mph in 2004.

Bobby Allison's violent crash in 1987, which sent debris flying into the stands, injuring several fans, led to the use of restrictor plates at Talladega and Daytona to limit the cars' power and speed. Dale Earnhardt holds the record for most Cup wins at the track, with 10.

39 THE BIG ONE

Most folks will tell you they don't go to a race to see the wrecks. And that's partly true, but a key component in the allure of racing is the potential for disaster. The combination of extreme speeds and unrelenting competition makes wrecks unavoidable. On superspeedways like Daytona and Talladega, with so many cars running together, a huge pileup is almost guaranteed. Under the assumption that it will happen sooner or later, drivers hope and pray that they aren't victimized by "the Big One."

40 RACING ACROSS THE SILVER SCREEN

The daring and excitement of stock car racing have been celebrated on the silver screen for nearly as long as the sport has been around. And some big names have had starring roles, such as Elvis Presley in *Speedway*, Burt Reynolds in *Stroker Ace*, Jeff Bridges in *The Last American Hero*, Tom Cruise and Robert Duvall in *Days of Thunder*, and Will Ferrell in *Talladega Nights*. The world premiere of the 2006 animated film *Cars* was held at Lowe's Motor Speedway, and featured the vocal talents of not only Owen Wilson and Paul Newman but also NASCAR legends Richard Petty, Darrell Waltrip, Dale Earnhardt Jr., and Humpy Wheeler.

> *"[Fans] don't want to see death.*
> *They want to see death defied."*
>
> —*Monte Dutton, from* Haul A** and Turn Left:
> The Wit and Wisdom of NASCAR

TWO-TIMERS

Mario Andretti and A. J. Foyt are the only two drivers ever to win both the Daytona 500 and the Indianapolis 500. Andretti won at Daytona in 1967, then at Indy in 1969. Foyt won the Indy 500 four times, in 1961, '64, '67, and '77, and added the Daytona 500 to his incredible résumé in 1972.

THE VOICE IN MY HEAD

Bobby Isaac won 37 times at NASCAR's top level, including 17 wins in 1969 and 11 more in 1970, driving the Harry Hyde-prepared K&K Insurance Dodge. He won his first and only points title in 1970, and set a closed-course speed record that same year when he was clocked at 201.104 mph at Talladega Superspeedway. Incredibly consistent, Isaac posted 170 top-ten finishes in just 308 starts.

In the 1973 Winston 500 at Talladega, Isaac inexplicably pulled off the track and into the pits while leading the race. He climbed out and quit the race, saying a voice in his head had told him to get out of the car. Isaac died a few years later, in 1977, from a heart attack he suffered after similarly pulling out of a Sportsman race in Hickory, North Carolina. He was named one of NASCAR's "50 Greatest Drivers of All Time" in 1998.

Miss USA Diana Batts kissing Mario Andretti, Daytona, 1967. Inset: A. J. Foyt, left, and Bobby Isaac

"If everything seems under control, you're just not going fast enough."
—Mario Andretti

THE ALABAMA GANG

Bobby Allison, his brother Donnie, and Red Farmer left Florida for the dirt tracks of Alabama in the late 1950s, setting up shop in Hueytown, on the outskirts of Birmingham. They soon began traveling throughout the Southeast, winning more than their share of races, and became known as "the Alabama Gang." As the years passed, Jimmie Means and Neil Bonnett joined the Gang, along with Bobby's son Davey and Hut Stricklin, who married Donnie's daughter, Pam. Hueytown's main street was renamed Allison-Bonnett Memorial Drive in the early 1990s in tribute to the Gang.

BOBBY ALLISON

Through 2007, only Richard Petty and David Pearson won more Cup races than the 84 Allison won in a career that stretched from 1961 to 1988. A five-time runner-up in the points championship, Allison put the crowning achievement on his career when he finally broke through and won his only Cup in 1983. A charter member of "the Alabama Gang," Allison won the Daytona 500 three times, in 1978, '82, and '88, which was his last Winston Cup victory, at the age of 50. Allison was voted NASCAR's Most Popular Driver six times. A violent crash at Pocono Raceway in 1988 left him with severe injuries that brought his Hall of Fame career to an end. Tragically, Allison also lost his sons Clifford and Davey in racing-related accidents. Allison was named one of NASCAR's "50 Greatest Drivers of All Time" in 1998.

"He loved to race more than any human being I've ever known."

—Humpy Wheeler on Bobby Allison, from The Wildest Ride: A History of NASCAR, by Joe Menzer

45 CALE

No other Cup driver bounced around from team to team as much as Cale Yarborough and still enjoyed the amazing success he had. Over the course of a career that lasted more than 30 years, Yarborough drove for some of the most notable teams in NASCAR history, including the Wood brothers, Bud Moore, Hoss Ellington, Junior Johnson, and Harry Ranier. Along the way, Yarborough won 83 Cup races and three Winston Cup championships. Those three championships came in consecutive years from 1976 to 1978, making Yarborough the only driver ever to win three straight Cup titles. He was particularly successful at Daytona and Darlington. He won the Daytona 500 four times, in 1968, '77, '83, and '84. And he had a record five wins in the Southern 500 at Darlington Raceway. In 1976, Yarborough set a modern-era record by winning five consecutive Cup races. Yarborough was named one of NASCAR's "50 Greatest Drivers of All Time" in 1998.

"I wanted to win that [third consecutive title] bad, because nobody else had ever done it."

—Cale Yarborough

46 BIG BROTHER TO THE RESCUE

The 1979 Daytona 500 was headed for yet another classic finish, with Cale Yarborough and Donnie Allison bumping and banging their way toward the checkered flag. With less than a lap to go, headed down the backstretch, Yarborough attempted to slingshot past Allison on the low side, but Allison went for the block. They bumped and Yarborough went into the infield grass. Yarborough tried to recover and shot back onto the track, slamming into Allison a few times, ultimately smashing him into the wall in Turn 3, wrecking both cars. Richard Petty and Darrell Waltrip flew right by third-place A. J. Foyt, who had slowed to avoid the mess, and Petty outraced Waltrip to the line to win his sixth Daytona 500. In the meantime, Donnie's older brother, Bobby Allison, stopped to offer Donnie a ride back to the garage. Words were exchanged with Yarborough, and suddenly Yarborough came after Bobby, hitting him with his helmet. A fight broke out, and Bobby Allison pummeled the smaller Yarborough on national television. It may not have been the kind of publicity NASCAR was looking for, but it certainly made many sit up and take notice of the sport.

"And that's when Cale commenced to beating on my fist with his face."

—Bobby Allison

Bobby Allison, left, exchanging pleasantries with Cale Yarborough, Daytona, 1979

47 BILL JR.

Bill France Jr. was only two years old in 1935 when his father packed him into the car and headed south to Florida. His future was about to change in a big way. As Big Bill built NASCAR into a major spectator sport, Bill Jr. worked an assortment of jobs in the family business, including selling tickets and concessions, and helping with the construction of Daytona International Speedway.

In 1972, Bill Jr. succeeded his father as president of NASCAR and over time became the most powerful figure in racing history—bringing in tremendous amounts of operating revenue through corporate sponsorships as well as radio and television broadcast deals. For more than three decades, Bill Jr. continuously expanded the reach of NASCAR, building the family business into a racing empire worth billions of dollars that includes ownership of more than a dozen racetracks. Mike Helton replaced France as NASCAR president in November 2000, but France remained on as chairman until October 2003. He passed away in 2007, leaving behind a legacy that will endure for generations to come.

"He is a hero in my eyes forever
for what he has done in the sport."

– Junior Johnson on Bill France Jr.

48 BENNY PARSONS

Parsons won 21 Cup races and one points championship over the course of his career, but that was only a small part of his legacy. He was one of the nicest and most genuine people you could ever want to meet. His smile was infectious, and his down-home, folksy, engaging nature was irresistible. So much so that when it looked as if Parsons was going to lose his shot at the 1973 Winston Cup championship after a wreck early in the season-ending American 500 at North Carolina Speedway in Rockingham, other crews shared parts and helped repair the car so that Parsons could get back in the race. Parsons finished 184 laps behind race winner David Pearson, but the remarkable and unprecedented show of sportsmanship and support by his competitors helped him to a 28th-place finish, earning Parsons enough points to edge Cale Yarborough for the championship. That pretty much says it all.

"If ever there was a person that should live forever, it should be BP."

—Bob Jenkins on Benny Parsons

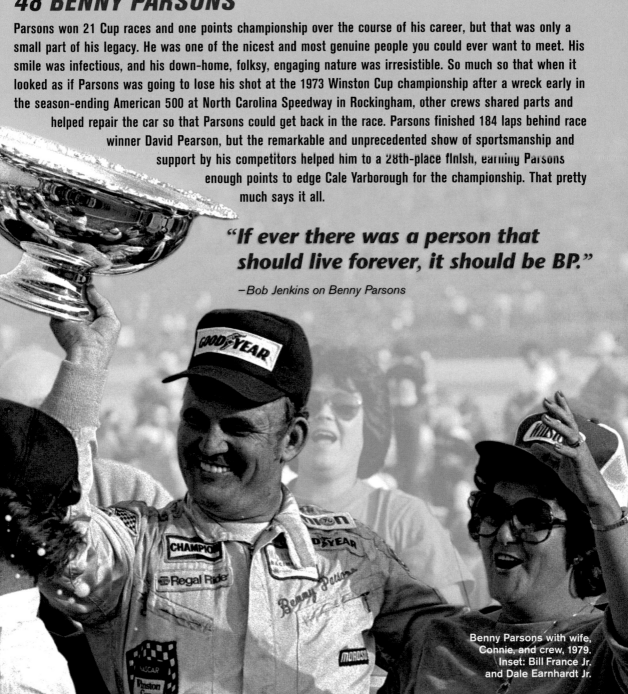

Benny Parsons with wife, Connie, and crew, 1979. Inset: Bill France Jr. and Dale Earnhardt Jr.

49 SLIP SLIDIN' AWAY

The finish of the 1976 Daytona 500 was even more dramatic than the Pearson-Petty duel down the stretch at the 1974 Firecracker 400. As the two cars took the white flag, Petty held a two-car-length lead heading into Turn 1. But Pearson closed the gap and was right on Petty's tail as the two cars came out of Turn 2 and headed down the backstretch. Pearson dove low and got past Petty as they entered Turn 3. Petty slid in behind Pearson and then went low himself as he tried to retake the lead. The two cars swapped a little paint, and Petty nosed past coming out of Turn 4. As Petty slid up the track in front of Pearson entering the tri-oval, he clipped the front of Pearson's car, sending them both spinning. Pearson bounced off the wall and slid into the infield grass. Petty hung on momentarily, then also crashed into the wall and spun his way down the tri-oval toward the finish line. He came to a stop in the grass just 100 yards or so from the finish line—but his car had stalled. As he desperately tried to recrank it, Pearson, who had managed to keep his car running by staying on the clutch, inched through the grass, climbed back onto the apron, and beat Petty to the checkered flag in one of the most memorable finishes ever.

David Pearson (21) struggling to cross the finish line ahead of Richard
Petty, in the grass, at the 1976 Daytona 500. Inset: David Pearson

Janet Guthrie

50 JANET GUTHRIE

Guthrie followed in Louise Smith's footsteps, becoming the first female driver to compete in a NASCAR Winston Cup event, in 1976 at Charlotte. She finished 15th. The following year, Guthrie made more history when she became the first woman to qualify for and drive in the Daytona 500, finishing 12th. Later that same year, she recorded her best finish in a Winston Cup event, finishing sixth at Bristol Motor Speedway.

51 THE START OF SOMETHING BIG

When Willie T. Ribbs was arrested for driving the wrong way on a one-way street in Charlotte, North Carolina, and missed a practice session, H. A. "Humpy" Wheeler, president of Charlotte Motor Speedway, and car owner Will Cronkite had to scramble to find a replacement driver for the 1978 World 600. Wheeler called on an ornery local kid who had earned a reputation for gutsy driving on the short tracks around the area. Just who was this untested youngster who would make his NASCAR debut in the series' longest race? Dale Earnhardt.

"You drive the car, you don't carry it."

–Janet Guthrie

52 THE GRAY GHOST

Buddy Baker, son of stock car legend Buck Baker, won 19 Cup races from 1959 through 1992, which included NASCAR's version of the career "Grand Slam"—the Daytona 500, the Winston 500 (now called the Aaron's 499), the Coca-Cola 600, and the Southern 500.

When Baker finally won the Daytona 500 in 1980, on his 18th try, the car he drove featured a paint scheme that caused it to blend in with the track, making it hard to see. Driving the No. 6 Dodge known as "the Gray Ghost," Baker recorded the fastest average winning speed in the history of the Great American Race: 177.602 miles per hour.

Baker later went on to become a commentator for television broadcasts of NASCAR races. He was named one of NASCAR's "50 Greatest Drivers of All Time" in 1998.

53 NICE SHOES

Dave Marcis holds the record for consecutive starts in the Daytona 500 with 32, the last in 1999. He never won the race. In fact, Marcis, who preferred wearing wing-tipped shoes when he raced, won only five times in 883 career Cup starts, but he continued to race for 20 more years after his last victory, in 1982.

> *"We have done so much with so little for so long that now we can do anything with nothing."*
>
> –Dave Marcis

Buddy Baker celebrating a victory with a couple of racestoppers

"With ten to go, I didn't have a code of ethics."

–Buddy Baker

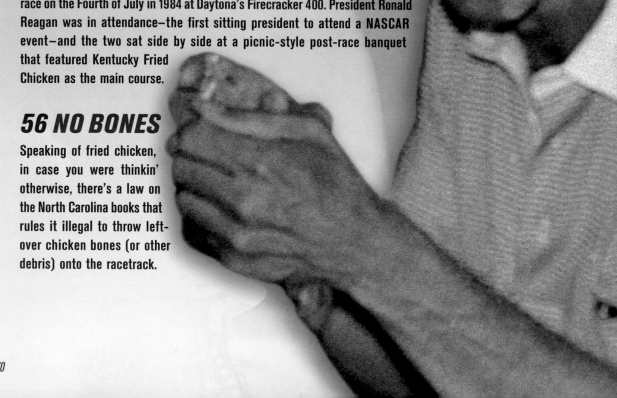

54 SEVENTH HEAVEN

You can give Richard Petty's crew chief Dale Inman a great deal of credit for the success the team had for so many years. The cousins grew up together in Randleman, North Carolina, and when Petty began his racing career, Inman was there fine-tuning his cars. One of the best moves made by Inman, in a career filled with pivotal strategic decisions, was his choice to just put fuel in Petty's car as he pitted with 25 laps left in the 1981 Daytona 500. Petty entered the pits in fifth place, but his quick gas-and-go stop got him out of the pits well ahead of his competition who all took on new tires and fuel. Petty led the rest of the way and won his record seventh Daytona 500.

55 NUMBER 200

It took some time, but Richard Petty finally won his history-making 200th Cup race on the Fourth of July in 1984 at Daytona's Firecracker 400. President Ronald Reagan was in attendance—the first sitting president to attend a NASCAR event—and the two sat side by side at a picnic-style post-race banquet that featured Kentucky Fried Chicken as the main course.

56 NO BONES

Speaking of fried chicken, in case you were thinkin' otherwise, there's a law on the North Carolina books that rules it illegal to throw left-over chicken bones (or other debris) onto the racetrack.

Richard Petty and President Ronald
Reagan enjoying some fried chicken
after Petty's 200th Cup victory in 1984

57 DAVEY ALLISON

Son of NASCAR legend Bobby Allison, Davey Allison qualified second for the Daytona 500 in his rookie season of 1987, making him the only rookie to start on the front row of NASCAR's biggest race. He went on to win two races that year and the Rookie of the Year award. Allison won five times in 1991 and 1992, including his first and only victory in the Daytona 500, in 1992. He tallied 19 Cup wins in less than seven full seasons before tragedy struck.

On the verge of becoming the sport's next superstar, Allison died of injuries he sustained when the helicopter he was piloting crashed while attempting to land at Talladega Superspeedway in 1993. His hometown of Hueytown, Alabama, paid tribute to Allison by naming a local street Davey Allison Boulevard. NASCAR honored him in 1998 as one of the "50 Greatest Drivers of All Time."

58 BEST OF THE BEST

Lots of folks imagine that they can handle the speed and intensity of stock car racing, but only the very best have any chance of succeeding. What separates these drivers from the rest of the pack? It appears to be something that science has yet to find the ability to fully measure—a more acute awareness; a greater sense of one's surroundings; an ability to see what others don't or can't, possibly even at a slower speed than the rest of us. And of course, no fear—absolute courage where anything less will not get it done.

"[Allison] was young, wildly talented,
wildly successful, wildly adored by
sponsors—and wildly adored by fans."

—Joe Macenka

"I'm gonna make these folks forget all about Richard Petty."

—Darrrell Waltrip

59 DARRELL WALTRIP

Maybe Darrell Waltrip talked a little too much for his own good, but he backed up his words with his success on the track. Nicknamed "Jaws" by Cale Yarborough for his aggressive driving style and candid nature, Waltrip was one of the dominant drivers of his generation. He won three Winston Cup points titles driving for Junior Johnson, including back-to-back 12-win championship seasons in 1981 and 1982; his third title came in 1985.

It took a while, but Waltrip finally won the Daytona 500 on his 17th try, in 1989. He had a little more luck in the Coca-Cola 600 at Charlotte Motor Speedway, winning that race a record five times. Waltrip's 84 Cup wins tie him with Bobby Allison for third on the all-time list through 2007.

After retiring in 2000, Waltrip moved into the broadcast booth, where his exuberance and common use of racing vernacular add a lively and entertaining charm to the commentary. In his first race as an analyst for Fox in 2001, his brother Michael won the Daytona 500 as Darrell enthusiastically cheered him on.

60 GETTIN' IT DONE

Stock car racing is not just about the drivers and their cars. So much goes on behind the scenes at the shops and in the garages. Some of NASCAR's best, past and present, include engine builders and crew chiefs such as Ernie Elliott, Ray Evernham, Jeff Hammond, John Holman, Ralph Moody, Harry Hyde, Dale Inman, Chad Knaus, Buddy Parrott, and Greg Zipadelli. And owners like Richard Childress, Joe Gibbs, Rick Hendrick, Bud Moore, Roger Penske, Harry Ranier, Jack Roush, Robert Yates, and the Wood brothers.

61 OVER THE WALL

Many races are won and lost down on pit road. When a driver pulls into the pits, seven men go over the wall in a choreographed ballet of intense activity. The jack man, tire changers, tire carriers, gas man, and catch-can man all attempt to perform their tasks in perfect synchronicity in a matter of just a few seconds.

And pit strategy is just as important. The crew chief must decide when to bring in the driver, what adjustments to make, how many tires to take, how much gas is needed, and more. Making the right or wrong call can win or lose a race. No pressure.

"I'm just out there doing what I like to do."

–Bill Elliott

62 MILLION DOLLAR BILL

Few drivers in NASCAR history have ever been as popular as Bill Elliott. "Awesome Bill from Dawsonville" won the Most Popular Driver award a record 16 times between 1984 and 2002. His 44 wins through 2007 rank him 14th on NASCAR's all-time list, and include an 11-win season in just 28 starts in 1985—yet he finished second in the points championship to Darrell Waltrip. He twice won the Daytona 500, in 1985 and 1987. His No. 9 Coors Ford was so dominant in the 1985 race that nearly half the field failed to finish in a futile effort to keep pace.

Building on his season-opening victory at Daytona in 1985, Elliott came from two laps down to win the Winston 500 in Talladega, then took the checkered flag at Darlington later that same year in the Southern 500, making him the first driver to win the Winston Million, a $1 million bonus for winning three of four races designated as NASCAR's "Grand Slam." Elliott won his only Winston Cup points title in 1988 and was named one of NASCAR's "50 Greatest Drivers of All Time" in 1998.

63 THE PASS IN THE GRASS

The 1987 edition of NASCAR's annual All-Star race, which debuted in 1985, featured one of the most memorable moments in stock car racing history. In the 10-lap green flag sprint to the finish, the finale of a three-segment race, Bill Elliott, Geoff Bodine, and Dale Earnhardt battled for the lead as they entered the first turn. Elliott got into the back of Bodine and spun him. Earnhardt dove low and charged into the lead. After the restart, Elliott, who later insisted Earnhardt had initiated the contact, chased down Earnhardt. They bumped and banged their way around the track, swappin' paint as they came down the frontstretch on lap 3. Another bump from Elliott sent Earnhardt careening into the grass. The car slid sideways, but somehow, incredibly, he regained control and zoomed back onto the asphalt in front of Elliott. A few laps later, Earnhardt's yellow and blue No. 3 Wrangler Monte Carlo took the checkered flag, and a legend was born.

64 THE TIRE ON THE WALL

Dale Earnhardt's 0-fer streak in the Great American Race was at 11 when he arrived at Daytona in 1990. Richard Childress' team had the car running great all week as Earnhardt cruised to victory in Thursday's 125-mile qualifying race, and Earnhardt was finally poised to win his first Daytona 500 with one lap to go. But a piece of debris cut the right rear tire on the Goodwrench No. 3 coming out of Turn 2. As the tire slowly went flat, Earnhardt's car shot up the banking and Derrike Cope rocketed past and took the checkered flag for his first Winston Cup victory. The incident was so gut-wrenching to car owner Richard Childress that he took the shredded tire back to his shop and hung it on the wall as a painful reminder that a race is never over until the checkered flag drops.

"Don't come here and grumble about going too fast. Get the hell out of the race car if you have feathers on your legs or butt."

—Dale Earnhardt

Geoff Bodine (11) leads Dale Earnhardt (3) down the frontstretch at the start of the 1990 Daytona 500

65 THE INTIMIDATOR

Richard Petty may be the King of stock car racing, but Dale Earnhardt is without a doubt the most revered driver in the sport's history. To say Earnhardt's driving style was aggressive is an understatement. He was unrelenting on the track, and just the sight of him in the rearview mirror often unnerved other drivers. He was absolutely unafraid of nudging, pushing, or bumping others out of his way and completely unapologetic about it. The track belonged to him, and you had better be faster than him or get the hell out of the way.

Earnhardt won 76 races over the course of his career, including an 11-win season in 1987, and won seven points championships along the way, tying him with Richard Petty for the most ever.

Earnhardt died tragically in a final lap crash at the 2001 Daytona 500. Michael Waltrip and Dale Earnhardt Jr., members of Earnhardt's team, finished first and second in that race. Fans continue to mourn the loss of "the Intimidator," and his famed No. 3 is still displayed in tribute by countless devoted fans.

"You win some, you lose some, you wreck some."

—Dale Earnhardt

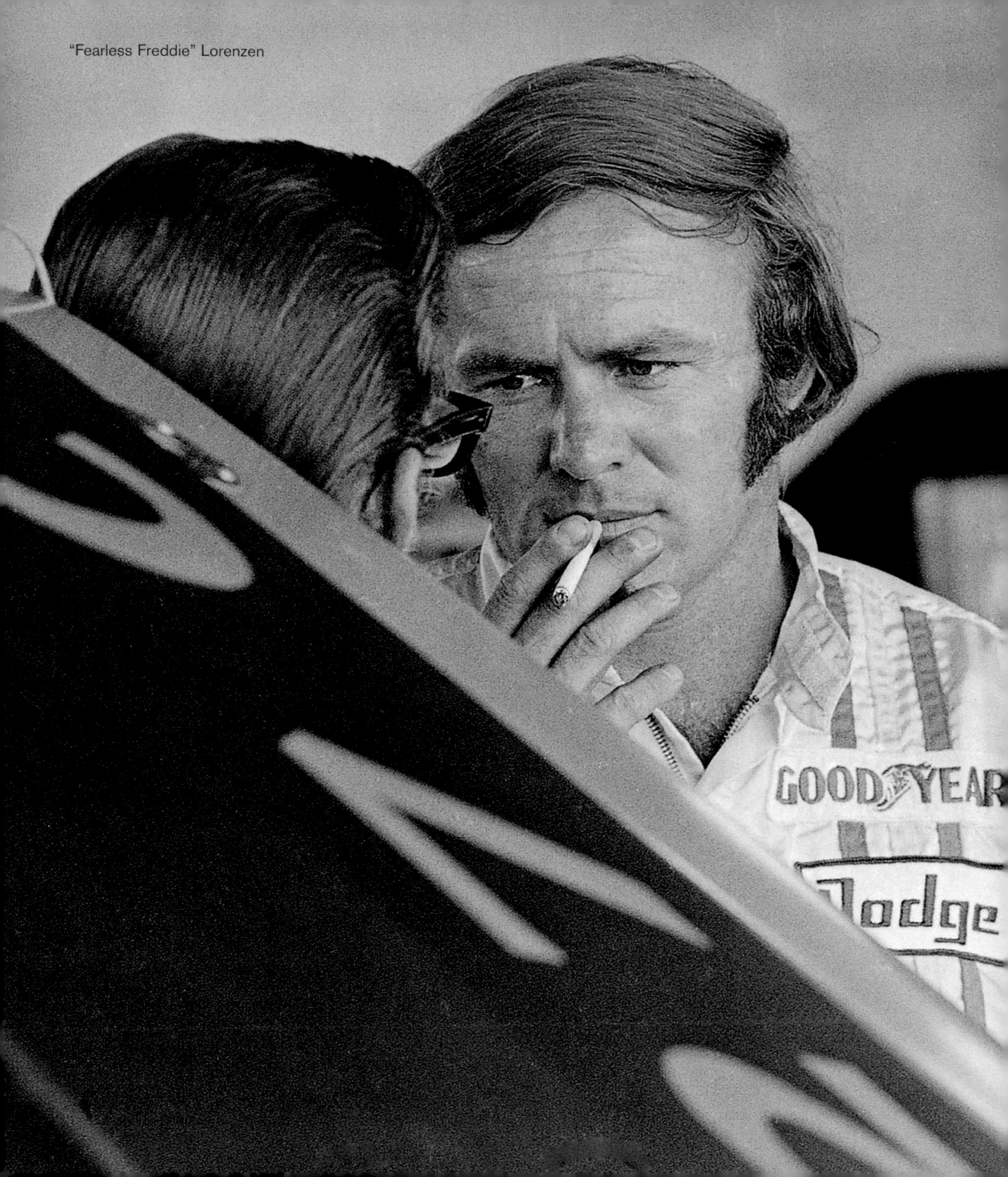

"Fearless Freddie" Lorenzen

66 HANDSOME HARRY

"Handsome Harry" Gant had one magical September in 1991. Gant won every race that month—four in a row, tying a modern-era record at the age of 51—earning him the nickname "Mr. September." His hometown of Taylorsville, North Carolina, raised a green and white No. 33 "Skoal Bandit" flag in the center of town each time he won. It flew for 29 straight days.

67 GREAT NAMES

"The King," "the Intimidator," "the Silver Fox," "Million Dollar Bill," and the "Rainbow Warriors" are some of the most recognizable nicknames in NASCAR, but how about these: "Chargin'" Charlie Glotzbach, "Coo Coo" Marlin, Ernie "Swervin' Irvan," "Fireball" Roberts, "Speedy" Thompson, "Handsome Harry" Gant, "Front Row Joe" Nemechek, "Big Track Jack" Sprague, "Buckshot" Jones, "Fearless Freddie" Lorenzen, and the "King of the Beach."

68 HUMPY WHEELER

H. A. Wheeler is one of the most influential men in NASCAR—a legend among legends. Growing up in Belmont, North Carolina, where his father coached football at the Belmont Abbey College, Wheeler found himself visiting local dirt tracks and quickly became hooked on racing.

Wheeler inherited his nickname, "Humpy," from his father, who earned it after he was caught smoking Camel cigarettes as a football player in college. Known as the "P. T. Barnum of racing," Wheeler's grand and often outrageous promotions have included reenacted military maneuvers complete with helicopter assaults and explosions, elephants at press conferences, and even dancing bears in response to a wry comment by a member of the media. He once considered staging a man-versus-shark battle to the death in front of the race crowd, though no one but Wheeler knows for sure if he was completely serious.

Named general manager of Charlotte (currently Lowe's) Motor Speedway in 1975, Wheeler and track owner Bruton Smith had lights installed at the speedway in 1992 so they could run races at night—a throwback to the early days. Wheeler's creative leadership made Lowe's Motor Speedway one of the best venues in stock car racing, and he continues to have a huge positive impact on the sport today.

69 UNDER THE LIGHTS

The first modern-era Cup race to be held under the lights was the Coca-Cola 600 at Charlotte Motor Speedway on May 16, 1992. Davey Allison took the checkered flag inches ahead of Kyle Petty, and big-time night racing was born.

Stuntman Mark Hager jumps his car through flames during pre-race entertainment at Lowe's Motor Speedway

DANGEROUSMOMENTS.COM

GER

517

COASTAL
TECHNICAL SERVICES, LLC

"Most people live their lives in gray or black and white. Maybe we bring a little Technicolor into their lives."

—Humpy Wheeler

70 RACIN' IN A CEREAL BOWL

The closest thing you'll find to old-time dirt track racing in NASCAR's Sprint Cup series is at the track known as "Thunder Valley USA," in Bristol, Tennessee. Tucked into the mountains in the northeast corner of the state, Bristol Motor Speedway is a half-mile of pure crazy. This little track is also one of the drivers' favorites. Spins and crashes are common in the arena-style setting as 43 cars fight for track position and the coveted checkered flag. Bristol hosts two Cup races a year, which are both fan favorites—especially the Sharpie 500, run at night, which sells out months in advance. Sterling Marlin once described the racing at Bristol "like racing fighter jets in a gymnasium."

71 THE POLISH VICTORY LAP

After Alan Kulwicki won the 1992 Winston Cup by only 10 points over Bill Elliott, he drove around Atlanta Motor Speedway backward (in reverse) while going clockwise on a track normally driven in a counterclockwise direction. Kulwicki dubbed his stunt the "Polish Victory Lap." When Rusty Wallace won the 1993 Food City 500 at Bristol Motor Speedway just days after Kulwicki was killed in a plane crash on his way to the race, Wallace paid tribute to the deceased driver by driving a Polish Victory Lap of his own.

"It's the Roman Colosseum of NASCAR."

—Dario Franchitti

RUSTY WALLACE

In his very first Winston Cup race in the Atlanta 500 in 1980, Wallace finished second, driving for Roger Penske's team—a pretty impressive start to an outstanding career. Wallace won Rookie of the Year honors in 1984, in the No. 88 Gatorade Pontiac owned by Cliff Stewart, and won his first Winston Cup race in 1986—the Valleydale 500 at Bristol Motor Speedway. In 1989, Wallace won his only points championship, besting good friend and rival Dale Earnhardt by just 12 points while racking up six race wins. His association with Miller Brewing began in 1990, initially as driver of the Miller Genuine Draft No. 2 car for Raymond Beadle. Wallace took the sponsorship with him when he returned to Penske Racing in 1991, winning a career-high 10 races in 1993.

Wallace was at his best on the short tracks, notching nine career wins at Bristol and seven more at Martinsville. He won at least one Cup race for 16 consecutive seasons, from 1986 to 2001—the third-longest streak of all time. Wallace raced his final season in 2005 and moved into the broadcast booth in 2006, covering races for ABC and ESPN. He was named one of NASCAR's "50 Greatest Drivers of All Time" in 1998.

"I'm proud of what I've done and I'm going out on top of my game."

—Rusty Wallace

JEFF GORDON

Born in California and raised in Indiana, Jeff Gordon was considered by many to be an outsider and too young when he joined NASCAR's ranks in 1992 at the tender age of 21. But "the Kid" quickly silenced his critics, winning the 1993 Rookie of the Year award, and then claimed his first Cup race win in 1994 at the Coca-Cola 600 at Charlotte Motor Speedway. He also won the inaugural Brickyard 400 that year, just a short drive from where he had grown up racing Midget cars.

Gordon won his first Winston Cup championships in 1995, and in 1997 he became the youngest driver to win the Daytona 500, at only 25 years old. His team was nicknamed the "Rainbow Warriors" for the vivid, multi-colored No. 24 DuPont Chevrolet he drove. In 1998, Gordon had his best season, and one of the best in NASCAR's modern era, when he won a record-tying 13 Cup races, giving him three consecutive seasons of 10 or more wins and his second consecutive points title. Gordon recorded his fourth Cup championship in 2001. Along the way, he has accumulated more than 80 Cup career wins, ranking him among the best drivers in the history of the sport.

A BEGINNING AND END

When Richard Petty raced for the last time, at the Hooters 500 in Atlanta in 1992, ending his historic 35-year career, another driver, looking to make a little bit of his own history, was making his NASCAR debut. His name was Jeff Gordon. Just six years later, NASCAR named Gordon one of the "50 Greatest Drivers of All Time."

DALE JARRETT

Son of racing legend Ned Jarrett, Dale had some big shoes to fill if he was going to follow in his father's footsteps. Many considered the younger Jarrett to have a future as a professional golfer, but he wanted to race. He built his own cars and eventually made it to NASCAR's premier division, where he proved himself after years of struggles on the short tracks. Jarrett won more than 30 times at the Cup level, including the 1993 Daytona 500, with his father calling the race for the national television audience. Jarrett won the Daytona 500 again in 1996, along with the Coca-Cola 600 and the Brickyard 400. He won his only Cup points title in 1999 with Robert Yates racing, and he added a third Daytona 500 in 2000. Named one of NASCAR's "50 Greatest Drivers of All Time" in 1998, Jarrett retired as a driver in 2008.

76 KISSING THE BRICKS

It has become a tradition that the winner and crew of NASCAR's annual 400-miler at Indianapolis Motor Speedway, known as the Brickyard, kneel and kiss the brick-paved finish line after the race. This tradition was started by Dale Jarrett and his Robert Yates Racing team when they won in 1996.

Dale Jarrett. Inset: Tony Stewart kissing bricks at Indianapolis Motor Speedway

Kevin Harvick (29) edges Mark Martin (01) at the finish of the 2007 Daytona 500.
Inset: Mark Martin

77 MR. CONSISTENCY

He never won a points championship or the Daytona 500. Still, Mark Martin is one of the most competitive and popular drivers in the history of NASCAR, earning him the nickname "Mr. Consistency." Since running his first Cup race in 1981, Martin has recorded 35 wins, putting him in the top 20 on the all-time list. His first victory came in 1989 at Rockingham, driving for Jack Roush, and his best season was 1998, when he won seven races, with 26 top-tens in 33 starts. He finished second to Jeff Gordon in the points race that year, one of four times Martin was runner-up for the Cup. In 2007, in one of the most memorable Daytona 500s in history, Martin was edged at the finish line by Kevin Harvick by a mere .02 seconds, denying him his first victory in NASCAR's biggest race. Martin holds the all-time record for wins in the Nationwide (formerly Busch) Series with 47 wins through 2007. He was named one of NASCAR's "50 Greatest Drivers of All Time" in 1998.

Dale Earnhardt taking the checkered flag at the 1998 Daytona 500. Inset: The reception line on pit road

78 QUITE A RECEPTION

It got to the point that it seemed to just about everyone, including Dale Earnhardt himself, that as great as he was, he might never win the Daytona 500. Poor pit stops, cut tires, blocked fuel lines—all kinds of stuff—had ruined his day time and again at Daytona. So when he led the 1998 race with just a few laps to go, it was almost as if everyone expected something to go wrong. And, sure enough, with just two laps left, there was a crash in Turn 2. But it happened behind Earnhardt, and he outraced Bobby Labonte to the checkered flag to win his first and only Daytona 500—on his 20th try! Seemingly everyone down in the pits lined pit road in a half-mile salute to "the Intimidator" as he made his way to Victory Lane.

Fans holding up three fingers in tribute to Dale Earnhardt

79 TRAGEDY AND TRIUMPH

While the 2001 Daytona 500 will forever be remembered as the race that ended with Dale Earnhardt's tragic death, it should also be remembered that Michael Waltrip, driving in his inaugural race for Earnhardt's Dale Earnhardt Inc. team, won for the first time in 463 tries. A true testament of perseverance if there ever was one.

80 THE THREE-FINGER SALUTE

After Dale Earnhardt's death, fans began what has become a tradition of holding up three fingers as cars pass by on the third lap of each race—a silent tribute to the great driver.

81 JEFF'S TRIBUTE

Jeff Gordon has tons of fans, but he also has tons of haters. A large contingent of NASCAR's faithful has never warmed to Gordon's more cosmopolitan style. When Gordon won his 76th Cup race, in Phoenix in 2007, he tied NASCAR-legend Dale Earnhardt for sixth on the all-time wins list. In a tribute to Earnhardt, Gordon stopped and picked up a flag bearing Earnhardt's famed No. 3, which he waved as he drove a slow victory lap around the track. More than a few fans were unhappy with Gordon's display, finding it offensive, and threw various items at his car as he passed. However, Earnhardt's son Dale Jr. was more gracious and was among the first drivers to greet and congratulate Gordon when he arrived in Victory Lane.

"Holding that 3 flag, it's certainly by no means saying we're as good as him. I learned so much from him. We wanted to honor him."

—Jeff Gordon

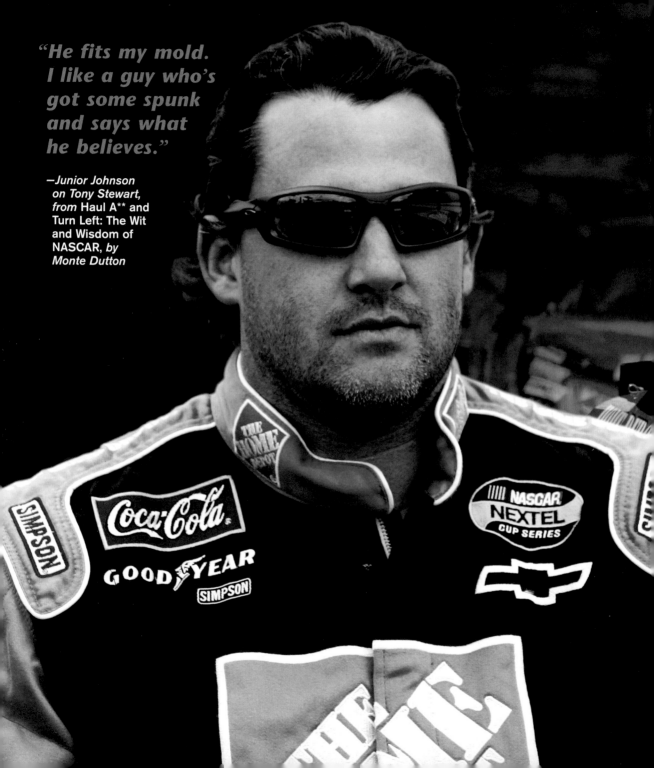

"He fits my mold. I like a guy who's got some spunk and says what he believes."

—*Junior Johnson on Tony Stewart, from* Haul A** and Turn Left: The Wit and Wisdom of NASCAR, *by Monte Dutton*

82 SMOKE

Tony Stewart is a throwback to the drivers of NASCAR's early years—hard-nosed, aggressive, and willing to speak his mind. He won NASCAR's Rookie of the Year award in 1999, a season that included three wins and a "double duty" day in May when he became the first driver to complete both the Indianapolis 500 and the Coca-Cola 600 in the same day. Since then, the man known as "Smoke" has won two point titles, in 2002 and 2005, while amassing more than 30 career wins. Many consider Stewart the best driver of his time. His orange-clad No. 20 Home Depot team is one of the most popular and recognizable teams in the sport today.

Tony Stewart, left, and Kurt Busch swap paint

83 SWAPPIN' PAINT

Much of the excitement in stock car racing comes from the drivers' willingness to race side by side. Of course, this can lead to some contact, both accidental and intentional. When cars bump and rub up against one another like this, it's called "swappin' paint."

And that's just one of the many colorful phrases used to describe the action. Here are a few more:

BACKMARKER: a driver who consistently spends much of the time at or near the back of the field

CHROME HORN: from the early days when race cars still sported chrome bumpers, the practice of tapping the car just ahead to get a driver's attention

COOPITITION: cooperation + competition, refers to two or more rivals working together for their mutual benefit

GETTING HUNG OUT TO DRY: losing lots of ground by moving or falling out of the draft

HAPPY HOUR: the final hour of practice, when drivers and crews fine-tune their cars for the upcoming race

LUCKY DOG: the first car one lap down when a caution flag comes out gets to move past the race leader and onto the lead lap

PUCKER VALUE: the intensity of a scary moment on the track

84 THE CHASE

In an effort to make late-season races more compelling,
NASCAR, led by CEO Brian France, decided to institute a playoff-style
format to the season-long points championship in 2004. After the first 26 Cup races,
only the top 10 drivers in points qualified for the Chase. Points were reset, and those 10 drivers
battled through the final 10 races of the season to determine the Series champion. While the format
wasn't universally embraced, it proved quite effective at generating the kind of race-to-the-wire excitement
NASCAR was looking for as Kurt Busch edged Jimmie Johnson by a razor-thin eight points in the very first
year. NASCAR expanded the Chase field to include the top 12 drivers in 2007.

It's hard enough to maintain control of an 800-plus horsepower race car when you're in "clean air" with no one nearby, but try keeping it together when cars stack up three and four wide with no room to spare. Now, that's racin'!

86 JUNIOR

Dale Earnhardt Jr. is by far the most popular driver in NASCAR today—and one of the most unassuming superstars around. From 1999 to 2007, "Junior" drove the Budwesier No. 8 Chevrolet for DEI, the race team founded by his legendary father, Dale Earnhardt. Nicknamed "Little E" early in his career, Junior won the Rookie of the Year award in 2000, following up two consecutive Busch Series titles in 1998 and 1999.

In 2001, he finished second to teammate Michael Waltrip at the season-opening Daytona 500, only to lose his father in a tragic final-lap crash. When NASCAR returned to Daytona in July, Earnhardt Jr. thrilled fans by winning the Pepsi 400. Junior has been most successful in restrictor-plate races at the big superspeedways. He won four consecutive races at Talladega from 2001 to 2003. In 2004, he added the Daytona 500 to his already impressive résumé.

87 HAVE A BEER

In the basement of Dale Earnhardt Jr.'s house—a little place he likes to call "Club E"—sits a cooler that holds 11 cases of beer. That's almost 300 cold ones. Anybody thirsty?

Dale Earnhardt Jr., right, celebrates his victory
in the 2000 Winston with his father

"I'm just going to keep driving
and have a good time doing it."

—Dale Earnhardt Jr.

88 THE DREAM TEAM

In 2007, Dale Earnhardt Jr. announced he was leaving the DEI team to join Hendrick Motorsports. It was a move questioned by many, but deemed necessary by Junior to achieve his goal of winning a Cup points championship. And it was huge in other ways. Not only was Junior leaving the family team and a relationship with Budweiser that had generated millions and millions of dollars in merchandise sales, but he was also joining archrivals Jeff Gordon and Jimmie Johnson—two drivers his loyal fans had come to despise over the years. The four-driver team, which also includes emerging star Casey Mears, is called "the dream team."

89 RACE CITY, USA

More than 60 race teams call the small town of Mooresville, North Carolina, home, including Dale Earnhardt Inc., Penske Racing South, and even Petty Enterprises, which relocated there after 60 years in Level Cross, North Carolina. Many of the top drivers live in town or nearby. It has become a destination for NASCAR fans looking to tour race shops and maybe get a glimpse of a popular driver. The town has even trademarked the name.

"Everywhere you go in Mooresville you see the residents and businesses celebrating our sport."

—Dave Marcis

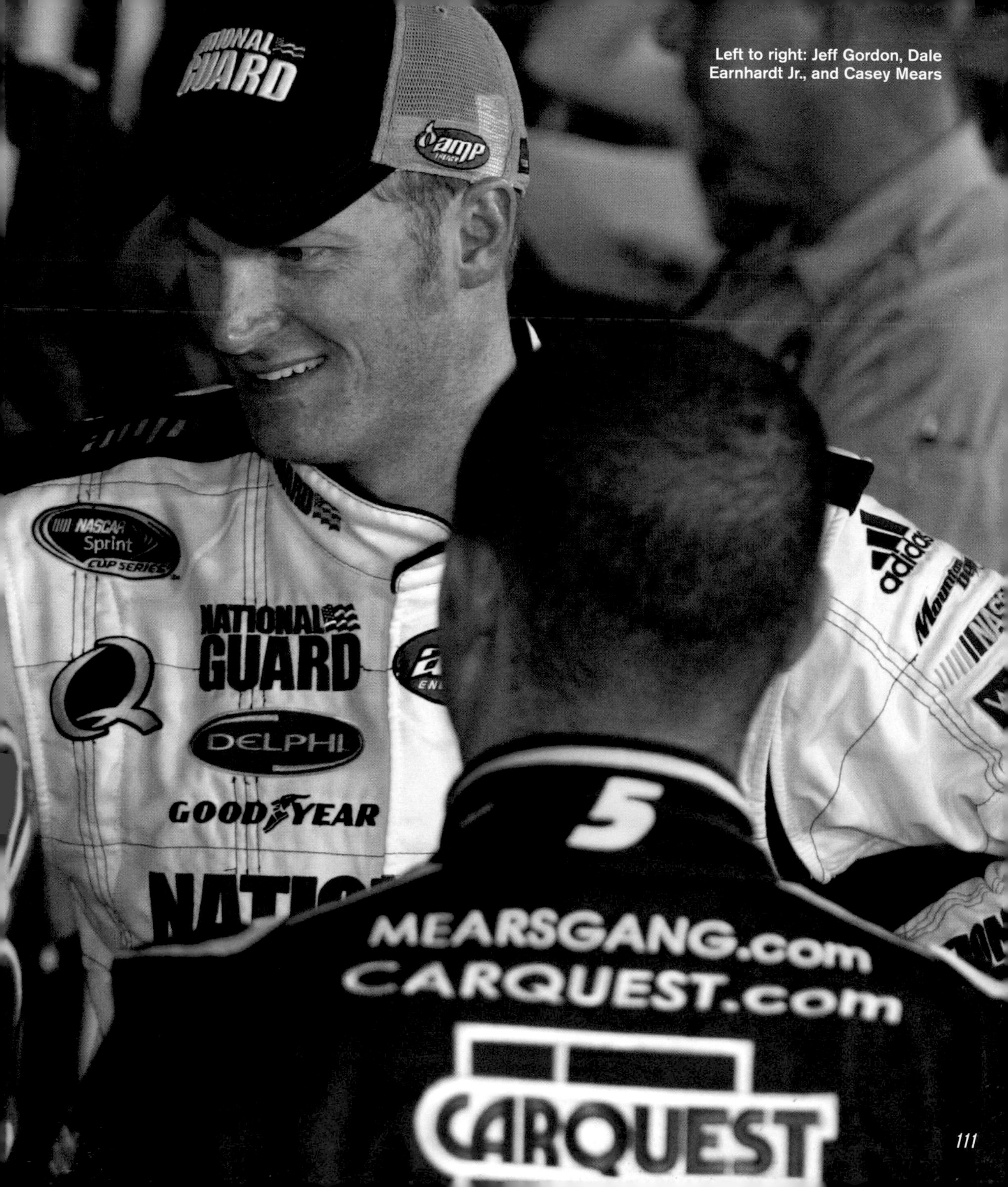

Left to right: Jeff Gordon, Dale Earnhardt Jr., and Casey Mears

JIMMIE JOHNSON

Johnson grew up in California racing motorcycles, winning his first championship at the age of eight—and the titles just kept coming. He drove his first Busch Series race in 1998, got his first win in Chicago in 2001, and drove his first Winston Cup race later that year at Lowe's Motor Speedway, finishing 15th.

With Hendrick Motorsports teammate Jeff Gordon acting as mentor, Johnson, driving the No. 48 Lowe's Chevrolet, quickly developed into one of NASCAR's best drivers, finishing second in points in both 2003 and 2004. Johnson won his first Cup championship in 2006, which included victories in the Daytona 500, the Allstate 400 at the Brickyard in Indianapolis, and the All-Star race—the first time a driver has won all three races and the Cup in the same year. He became the first driver to win back-to-back championships since Jeff Gordon in 1997 and 1998 when he won his second title in 2007. Johnson secured the 2007 Cup by winning four consecutive Chase races leading up to the finale at Homestead-Miami Speedway, tying the modern-era record for consecutive wins.

"If it's meant to be,
it's meant to be."

–Jimmie Johnson

91 WAVING THE WHITE FLAG

Many NASCAR tracks also host private events. In fact, it's not unusual for couples to get married at the track. Some brides wear the traditional white gown and veil, while others dress in the colors of their favorite driver. Often, vows are exchanged at the start-finish line. It kind of makes you wonder, just which one is it—start or finish? Maybe they should wave the white flag, you know, in surrender.

92 LOVE AMERICAN STYLE

During the 2008 NASCAR season, Office Depot, sponsor of Carl Edwards' No. 99 Ford Fusion, teamed up with Harlequin Enterprises, publisher of romance novels, to hold a contest in which the contest's winner had his or her marriage proposal featured on the back of Edwards' car during the 2008 Sprint Cup Series All-Star Challenge. Nothing says, "I love you," like a decal plastered on the rear end of a race car traveling at 180 miles per hour.

Carl Edwards in the No. 99 car.
Inset: A wedding at Bristol Motor Speedway

Ashley Judd, actress and wife of driver Dario Franchitti, strolls through the infield at Daytona

93 THE CHANGING DEMOGRAPHIC

After his victory at the 2003 Checker Auto Parts 500 in Phoenix, Dale Earnhardt Jr. was politely answering questions in the media center when a female fan sauntered up to a window nearby and lifted her shirt, exposing her assets for him and several members of the media to admire. Junior glibly commented to the media, "I guess the demographic of the sport is changing."

94 THE EXPANDING UNIVERSE

Stock car racing now extends far beyond its Southern roots, with Cup races in Indianapolis, Chicago, Phoenix, and even Las Vegas. The Nationwide Series holds races in Mexico and Canada. This impressive expansion has attracted some of the best drivers from open-wheel racing, including recent converts Dario Franchitti, Sam Hornish Jr., Juan Pablo Montoya, and Jacques Villaneuve.

95 ON TOP OF THE WORLD

NASCAR fan Patrick Hickey climbed Mount Everest in 2007. While on the mountain he kept a blog, which allowed him to monitor the progress of his favorite driver, Jeff Gordon, during the 2007 Nextel Cup season. One of the blog's readers contacted NASCAR officials to tell them about Hickey's expedition. Impressed with his drive and devotion to the sport, NASCAR sent a Nextel Cup flag halfway around the world, where the pilot of a rescue helicopter delivered it to Hickey at base camp, some 17,600 feet above sea level. Hickey carried the small flag up the mountain and planted it among all the Tibetan prayer flags that adorn the summit—on top of the world.

96 ICE TIME

NASCAR veteran Geoff Bodine's nonprofit organization, the Bo-Dyn Project, builds bobsleds for the U.S. Olympic team. Since 2006, a number of fellow drivers have ventured to the Olympic training facility in Lake Placid, New York, each winter to compete against one another on the ice in the Bodine Bobsled Challenge, which helps finance the project.

Boris Said pilots bobsled. Inset: Patrick Hickey on the summit of Mount Everest, 2007

"When I got to the top, it was beautiful to look down. From where I stood, there was nowhere left on earth to go."

–Patrick Hickey on climbing Mount Everest

97 THE BURNOUT

It has become commonplace in stock car racing for the winning driver to celebrate by smoking the tires in what's known as a "burnout." Different drivers have different styles. Some do doughnuts and figure eights while holding down the brake and spinning the rear tires. Others put the nose of the car against the wall and rev the engine. And some like it more freestyle. As long as it generates lots of smoke, it's all good.

98 SIPPING POINTS

If you pay attention at the end of a race as the winning driver emerges from his car after arriving in Victory Lane, you'll notice he's promptly handed a drink of one kind or another to gulp as the cameras record the celebration. This practice, like so much else in NASCAR, is done for the benefit of the corporate sponsors and is known as earning "sipping points."

99 THE HAT DANCE

Believe it or not, there is a standard set of procedures for what happens in Victory Lane at the completion of a race. The lists run about 25 items long, beginning with getting the media to Victory Lane with 10 to 15 laps to go and ending with individual photos and one-on-one interviews. After the trophy presentation, the driver and team are photographed wearing a variety of sponsors' hats. This little number is called "the hat dance."

Jimmie Johnson celebates with a classic burnout

one unstable element.
A NEW MOVIE FROM HBO FILMS
HBO FILMS PRESENTS A BEACON PICTURES/SECTION EIGHT PRODUCTION A SCOTT Z. BURNS FILM "Pu-239"
KATE DOWD
TATIANA S. RIEGEL, A.C.E. LEO TROMBETTA, A.C.E.
STEVEN SODERBERGH GEORGE CLOONEY BEN COSGROVE JENNIFER FOX
TOM MEYER
PREMIERES NOVEMBER 17, 8PM HBO
beauty
Walgreens
CHAMPION 2007
IMPALA SS
07
MOOG
COMP
Edelbrock
WIX
CLEVITE

100 THE BIG CITY

Since 1981, NASCAR has held its annual postseason awards banquet in New York City. What started out as a modest dinner at Tavern on the Green has grown into a huge spectacle now known as Champions Week, highlighted by the top drivers slowly parading their cars through Midtown in front of thousands of fans. If only they'd let them race!

Kasey Kahne

VICTORY LANE

Jimmie Johnson

ACKNOWLEDGMENTS

This book would not be possible without the help of many, many people. First and foremost, I would like to thank all of the men and women who have been a part of stock car racing from its modest beginnings to now. Their courage and determination, and rich, vibrant personalities have made the sport the wildly popular and thrilling spectacle it is today.

To my parents, Ron and Beth Green, I am forever grateful for all you've given me. I cherish so many moments, including the summer afternoons we spent listening to the race on the radio while we washed the cars, and the delicious picnics of homemade fried chicken and biscuits my brother Ron and I took along with us whenever we spent the day in the grandstand at Charlotte Motor Speedway.

To Humpy Wheeler and Max Muhleman, thanks for taking the time to tell your stories.

To Ted Ciuzio at AP Images, Matt Germala and Jason Sundberg at Getty Images, Betty Carlan at the International Motorsports Museum, Kristi King at Talladega Superspeedway, Keith Waltz at Lowe's Motor Speedway, Jake Harris at Darlington Raceway, David Hart at Richard Childress Racing, Patrick Hickey, and Francis Flock, for your help in tracking down and providing the incredibly wonderful images in this book. You have my eternal gratitude.

To all the good people at the Richard Petty Driving Experience, wow! Thanks for your friendship, coaching, and professionalism. What a blast! Really, really terrific.

To my crew at Stewart, Tabori & Chang, a special word of thanks, especially to Ann Stratton and Jennifer Levesque, my brilliant editors. And to Mary Tiegreen, my friend and mentor, I am so grateful for this opportunity.

To Joe Macenka, I couldn't have done it without you. Thanks for tightening things up. We were a little loose there at the beginning.

To Richard Slovak, my spotter, nobody does it better.

To Tamera Green, my dear sister-in-law, thanks for "gittin' 'er done."

And to Mary, Savannah, Dakota, and Sam, you are one special team. Lap after lap, day after day, you're always there for me. And that's all anybody could ever really ask for.

A Tiegreen Book

Published in 2008 by Stewart, Tabori & Chang
An imprint of Harry N. Abrams, Inc.

Text copyright © 2008 David Green
Compilation copyright © 2008 Mary Tiegreen

Library of Congress Cataloging-in-Publication Data
Green, David, 1959-
   NASCAR: 101 reasons to love stock car racing /
David Green.
     p. cm.
   ISBN 978-1-58479-733-3
   1. NASCAR (Association)–Miscellanea. 2. Stock car
racing–United States–Miscellanea. I. Title.
GV1029.9.S74G73 2008
796.72–dc22
2008015755

Editor: Ann Stratton
Designer: David Green, Brightgreen Design
Production Manager: Tina Cameron

All photos courtesy of AP Images except the following:

Pages 13 (postcard) and 85 (decal) courtesy of David Green

Pages 14–19 courtesy of Getty Images

Page 118 (inset) courtesy of Patrick Hickey

The text of this book was composed in Berthold Akzidenz Grotesk, ITC Stone Sans, and Sabon.

Printed and bound in China
10 9 8 7 6 5 4 3 2 1

HNA
harry n. abrams, inc.
a subsidiary of La Martinière Groupe

115 West 18th Street
New York, NY 10011
www.hnabooks.com